The Northamptonshire Way
An End to End of the County

by Mountain Bike

Vince Major

Published by Vince Major
Publishing partner: Paragon Publishing, Rothersthorpe
2nd edition

ISBN 978-1-78222-721-2

Book design, layout and production management by Into Print
www.intoprint.net
01604 832149

Cover photo
Location: Geddington Chase
Riders: Matt Earl, Shane Miller and Sam Piercey

Disclaimer
Every effort has been made to achieve accuracy of information for use in this guidebook. The author and publisher can take no responsibility or liability for any loss (including fatal), damage or trespass as a result of the route information or advice offered in this guidebook.

The inclusion of a path or track in this guide does not guarantee it remains a right of way. If conflict with a landowner occurs, please leave by the shortest possible route available and inform the relevant authority if deemed necessary.

Please follow the country code and always give way to pedestrians and horses.

CONTENTS

OVERVIEW

The Northamptonshire Way starts at the south western end of the county bordering Oxfordshire and heads north-east to traverse the whole length of this elongated county to finish just over the border in Cambridgeshire. Great views of the 'Rose of the Shires' can be had throughout the journey with highlights being the large expanses of Pitsford Water and the historical Rockingham Forest area.

A rolling route seeking out the best trails Northamptonshire has to offer includes single and doubletrack bridleways and byways, purpose built cycle paths and woodland tracks.

This route would not be suitable for a complete novice but with a little experience and a reasonable level of fitness there should not be too many problems.

Map Overview

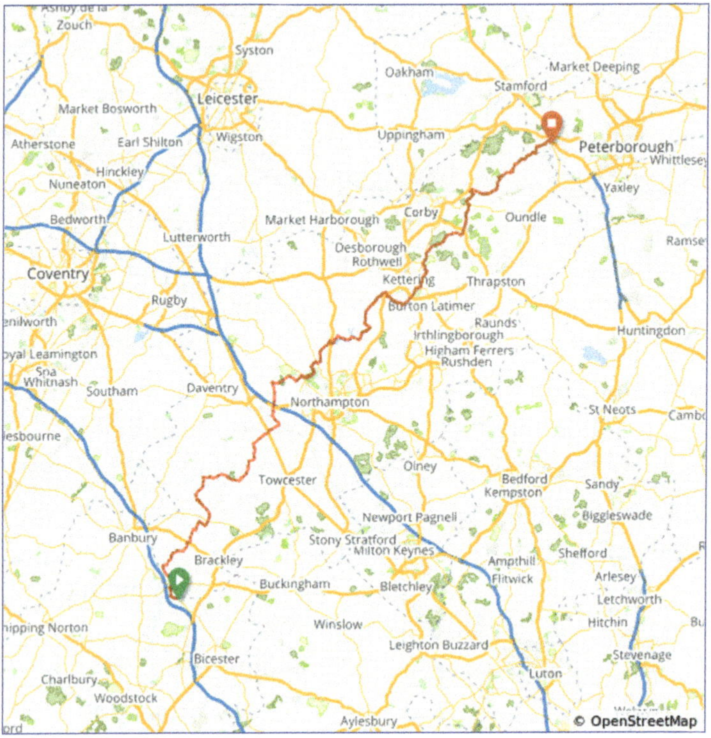

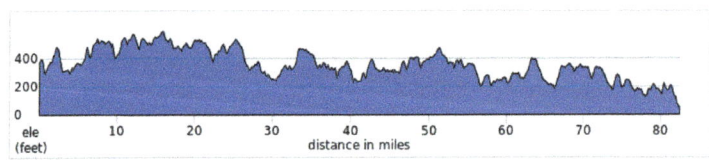

Elevation

HOW TO USE THIS BOOK

The main purpose of this guidebook is to provide the instructions to plot the route of 'The Northamptonshire Way' onto the relevant OS maps. The instructions for the route include many abbreviations which are listed in a table. The 6 figure grid reference numbers are compatible with the relevant OS Landranger 1:50,000 and OS Explorer 1:25,000 type maps. Some details for when you are on the route are also included in the route instructions when deemed necessary; these details are often useful when navigating through urban areas. Please note, plotting the route through towns and cities is difficult when using OS maps and so online mapping is recommended and is very useful for this purpose.

In the route instructions, 6 figure grid reference numbers and relevant abbreviations are all in **bold** lettering.

Other useful information is also included about bikes, kit, travel, accommodation, local bike shops, cafes and other shops en route.

KIT

The kit lists that follow will provide you with a rough idea of what you would need on a trip like this.

Bike

The ideal bike for this trip would be a lightweight, short-travel, full suspension mountain bike, 26, 27.5 or 29er. An equivalent hardtail would also be fine but not quite as comfortable. A mountain bike with more than 140mm travel is probably not that suitable. A CX/gravel bike would also be suitable but a hybrid type bike could only be used with good mud clearance and decent tyres.

Tubeless tyres or 'sealant' type tubes are a good idea to prevent punctures. Disc brakes are also a good option.

Whatever bike you choose, it needs to be in excellent working order because this route is hard on machinery especially if muddy.

Bike Spares

If you are attempting this ride unsupported then you are limited to what you can carry, though riding in a group means you can share the load.

If you have a support vehicle then bike spares are not an issue, just take everything!

Essentials for an unsupported trip will be:

- Tyre levers
- Spare tubes
- Tyre boot (for split tyre repair)
- Pump
- Patches
- Tubeless repair kit
- Multi-tool (inc. chain splitter & spoke key)
- Gaffer tape (wound around pump)
- Cable ties (various lengths)
- Mech hanger (specific to your bike)
- Gear cable
- Chain links/pins
- Small bottle of lube
- Rag
- Lightweight bike lock
- Small rear light

Clothing

It depends on the time of year and/or the forecast, but at the very least a good quality waterproof/windproof jacket.

If you are planning on carrying all your gear, on bike and après bike, then technical, lightweight materials are best.

Navigation

A GPS unit with the relevant mapping is a huge asset when tackling a ride like 'The Northamptonshire Way'. It's not essential to have a GPS but with the route uploaded onto the unit, it will save a lot of time out on the trail. GPX files can be found at **www.mtbepicsuk. co.uk/gps**.

However, you will still need the paper maps as they can often prove invaluable when you need the 'bigger picture' or to find an alternative route. Plus, they are great to look at when opened up to study the highlighted route.

OS Landranger 1:50,000 maps are recommended on this trip and generally have enough detail. The map numbers are: 141, 142, 151 & 152.

Please note:

The OS maps showing this route (PDF files) can be found on our website to download or print off. It's recommended to download them onto your smartphone where you can zoom in to enlarge details and not lose clarity. These files can be found at **www.mtbepicsuk.co.uk/maps**.

OS maps can also be borrowed from local libraries.

A compass and knowing how to use it is always worth having too!

First Aid Kit

As an experienced mountain biker you may know the basics of first aid, what should be in the kit and how to use it. It would be a good idea to read up and remind yourself of first aid procedures before the trip.

The most common problems encountered can be cuts, grazes, exposure, a broken or cracked collar bone, sunburn and saddle sores!

Miscellaneous

- A bladder type hydration system or bottles
- Lip balm
- Sunscreen (At least SPF 30)
- Chargers for GPS and phone
- Weatherproof bags (for phone and clothes etc.)

Please note:
These lists are not definitive and simply provide a pointer.

TRAVEL AND ACCOMMODATION

Logistics

'The Northamptonshire Way' can be ridden in either direction. A West to East crossing is used in the route description and instructions to take advantage of the often prevailing south-westerly wind.

There are many options of how to travel to and from the start and finish points of 'The Northamptonshire Way'.

Here are a few pointers:

Start at Souldern is just off the B4100, 4 miles north of junction10 on the M40

Finish at Wansford is next to the A1, west of Peterborough

- Travelling there in a support vehicle means having everything you need with you and a simple way to get home.
- Leave a vehicle at route finish and drive to start point.
- Nearest train stations to the start point (Souldern) is King's Sutton and the end point (Wansford) is Stamford or Peterborough
- Wansford Station (near Stibbington) is part of the Nene Valley Railway and is

approx. 2 miles from Wansford. This runs to and from Peterborough on a limited service using steam and diesel locos.

Trains

- www.nationalrail.co.uk
  The official source for UK train times, advance tickets and other information.

- www.thetrainline.com
  Phone app for times and fares.

- www.atob.org.uk
  Information on train companies and their policies on bike carriage.

- www.nvr.org.uk
  The Nene Valley Railway is a preserved railway running between Peterborough and Yarwell Junction.

Duration

Although not generally a super-technical route, to attempt this ride in a day would provide a decent challenge to any mountain biker. However, it would work well as a two or even a three day ride at a more leisurely pace and possibly take in some of the fantastic pubs en route!

Accommodation

There are B&B's and Guesthouses at the beginning and end points of this route and at the halfway point in the Pitsford/Brixworth area. There is also a large campsite near to Wansford - Yarwell Mill Camping and Caravan Park.

- -

THE NORTHAMPTONSHIRE WAY BY NUMBERS

- -

- 82 total miles (132km)
- 39 off-road miles (63km)
- 3,676ft total elevation gain (1,120m)
- 570ft highest point (174m)
- 22 off-road sections
- 1 town
- 24 villages
- 20 pubs en route

ROUTE DESCRIPTIONS

Souldern – Pitsford Water

38.05 total miles (61.2km)
14.75 off-road miles (23.73 km)
1,751ft elevation gain (534m)

Starting in Oxfordshire in the village of Souldern you will soon cross the county boundary at Ockley Brook ford into the south western tip of Northamptonshire.

An early off-road highlight is a long byway descent from Aynho that cumulates in another ford crossing. Another early highlight is the gradual descent towards Stuchbury which signals the start of semi-technical, often rutted trails with some particularly long sections near Moreton Pinkney. Quiet roads follow through several villages and on to another mainly off-road section to Nobottle, Upper Harlestone and Lower Harlestone, all of which are part of the Althorp Estate – the home and burial place of Princess Diana.

Then it's on to the epicentre of Northampton's mountain bike scene - Harlestone Firs, not a large area but packed with locally, purpose built quality singletrack. Then it's a quick blast along the Brampton Valley Way disused rail line and up locals' favourite, Merry Tom Lane, which leads to the scenic Pitsford Water and its excellent facilities that include a good bike shop and café.

Steep climb up to Nobottle Road

Pitsford Water - Wansford

37.16 total miles (59.8km)
19.49 off-road miles (31.35km)
1,475ft elevation gain (450m)

Ride the meandering bike trail along the northern shore of the reservoir to join quiet roads and byway sections that will take you through several villages and on to the only town on route – Kettering. Skirt through the south-east of the town, past local attraction Wicksteed Park and onto a mixture of bridleways, road and bike path to the historical village of Geddington which boasts a fine medieval bridge that crosses the River Ise. Next to the bridge is a ford that provides an interesting option to ride across if you wish!

A long section of byway through Geddington Chase follows, possibly the best section of the entire route, and leads into the large Rockingham Forest area in the north-east of the county.

This last part of 'The Northamptonshire Way' is mainly off-road and uses a variety of trails including several fine, fast descents on woodland tracks and stony bridleways. The county boundary is reached when entering the village of Wansford, and then end the route by crossing a picturesque section of the River

Nene to finish in the centre of the village in Cambridgeshire. There are a couple of pubs here if you wish to toast completing 'The Northamptonshire Way'...

Descent from Deenethorpe Airstrip

ROUTE INFORMATION

Bike Shops

* denotes bike shop on or within 10 minutes of route.

Broadribb Cycles
1 George Street
Banbury
OX16 5BH
01295 669065
OS Map 151
GR 458405

Broadribb Cycles
85 Sheep Street
Bicester
OX26 6JS
01869 253170
OS map 164
GR 584226

Leisure lakes Bikes
Abbey Retail Park
Daventry
NN11 4GL
01327 317158
OS Map 152
GR 574628

*Rutland Cycles
Brixworth Country Park
Brixworth
NN6 9DG
01604 881777
OS Map 152
GR 753695

*C&D Cycles
19 Montagu Street
Kettering
NN16 8XG
01536 411313
OS Map 141
GR 868789

Bristow's Cycles
46 Church Drive
Orton Waterville
Peterborough
PE2 5HE
01733 231755
OS Map 142
GR 157960

Shops en route

* denotes shop very close to route

- Kings Sutton – Co-op
- Greatworth – Village store
- Sulgrave – Village store
- Blakesley – Village store
- *Nether Heyford – Village store
- *Broughton – Co-op
- Kettering – Co-op
- *Brigstock – Co-op

Cafés en route

- Brixworth Country Park – The Willow Tree
- Geddington - Café Oak

TABLE OF ABBREVIATIONS

N	North
S	South
E	East
W	West
R	Right
L	Left
TR	Turn Right
TL	Turn Left
FR	Fork Right
FL	Fork Left
RH	Right Hand
LH	Left Hand
SA	Straight Ahead
SO	Straight Over
@	At
thru	Through
TJ	T Junction
Xroads	Crossroads
BW	Bridleway
BY	Byway
MR	Minor Road
NCN	National Cycle Network
SP	Sign Posted
MTB	Mountain Bike

ROUTE INSTRUCTIONS

Souldern - Pitsford Water

Start in the village of Souldern **@ 523315** and head **W** to join concrete doubletrack **BW** and cross Ockley Brook into Northants **@ 511318**. Head **N** on **BW** to join **MR** and continue to **TJ** with B4031. **TR** to **TJ** in Aynho then **TL** onto B4100 and **TR @ 512333** onto **MR** (Charlton Rd). Follow **SA** until, **@ 516336**, **TL** onto **BY** and descend to continue **SA** past farm and **thru** ford to bear **L** to join **MR @ 506347**. Follow to junction with **MR** and keep **SA** into Kings Sutton. Follow **SA** onto Wittall St then bear **R** onto Richmond St to pass shop and follow to bear **L** and exit village. Continue until **@ 508371**, **TR** onto metalled **BW**, bear **L** and follow **thru** farm buildings, then a quick **R L** will lead to track (**BW**) on field edge. Follow **thru** gap in hedge to diagonal track **thru** field up to corner of woodland **@ 514382**. **TR** onto good track then during descent, **TL** after hedge and descend to **TL thru** large gap in hedge (**BW**). Follow for 100m then **TR** across crop field (**BW**) to pick up hedge lined stony climb **@ 521385**. Follow **SA** to **MR** then **TL** and continue to **Xroads** in Farthinghoe. **TL** onto Queen St then **TR** onto Chapel Lane to **TJ** with A422. **TR** then **FL** onto

MR (Cockley Rd) **SP** Marston St Lawrence and follow **SA** until, @ **545417, TR** then **TL** towards Greatworth. Continue into Greatworth until just after pub on **R, TR** onto Helmdon Rd and follow until, @ **554428, TR** onto **BW** and continue to eventually meet gravel track @ **562422** then **TL** to **TJ** with B4525 @ **566428**.

TR then quickly **TL** to join **BY** and descend to cross stream @ **570437**. Continue **SA** then bear **L** past farm to join **MR** and follow to junction @ **567445. TL** and follow into Sulgrave until @ **557455, TL** then quickly **TR** onto Stockwell Lane (**BW**) next to shop. Follow **L** then **R** to eventually get to **MR** @ **550460. TR** then quickly **TL** to **TJ** in Culworth then **TR** to **TL** onto Barley Hill and follow to **TJ** @ **557478. TL** then after 600m at **RH** bend, **TL** and follow to old rail bridge @ **599494**. Cross bridge to **TR** onto track then bear **L** and continue **E** to eventually cross ford into Moreton Pinkney and on to **TJ** with **MR. TL** and continue **thru** village until just past village hall on **L**, @ **576494, FR** to soon join track. Follow to keep **SA** at staggered track junction @ **594495** to eventually meet **MR** @ **604490. TL** and follow **thru** Wood End and continue on to Blakesley. Head up High St and bear **R** at village green to **TJ**. Continue **SO** onto Church St and follow until, @ **635520 TL** and follow to **TJ** @ **637536. TL** and follow to **TJ** in Litchborough @ **633544. TR** (**SP** Bugbrooke) and follow to A5 **@ 657560**.

Continue **SO** A5 and bear **R** towards Bugbrooke. Follow under rail line, over canal, bear **L** then **TL** towards Nether Heyford. Continue into Nether Heyford until, **@ 662585**, **TR** onto Watery Lane and follow to **TJ**. **TR** and continue **SA** to **TJ @ 663597** . Cross **SO** to join track and head **N thru** several gates until doubletrack disappears at grassy field **@ 664621**. Keep **SA** across grassy field to a gate and continue on doubletrack to eventually climb steeply to **MR @ 661634**. **TR** and after 900m, **TL** and continue **E thru** Upper Harlestone until **@ 697635**, **TL** (SP Village Institute/ Playing Fields) and follow to **RH** bend **@ 701639** to join **BW** (effectively **SA**). Follow **BW SA thru** series of gates to A428 in Harlestone **@ 706645**. **TR** onto A428, continue past pub on **L** until, **@ 708642**, **TL** to join **BW** and follow round field edges into Harlestone Firs. Go **thru** the gate and up to trail **Xroads @ 714642**, **TL** onto wide track (**BW**) and bear **R** to track **TJ @ 717644**. **TL** then quickly **TR** onto wide track (**BW**), then **TL @** track **Xroads** and descend **SA thru** tunnel under rail line to follow **SA** up **thru** golf course to **BW** junction **@ 725649**. **TL** and follow to golf club car park entrance and continue **SA** to **MR @ 720658**. **TR** and follow until, **@ 723661**, **TL** onto **BW** and follow to track **TJ**. **TL** then quickly **TR** across crop field keeping **SA** to join one-way system to **TJ** with A5199. **TR**, then **TL @ Xroads** onto Pitsford Rd (**SP** Pitsford) and follow until **@ 735666**, **TL thru** railway/pub entrance to join Brampton Valley Way (**NCN** 6) and head **N** to next junction **@ 733680**. **TR** and follow good track (Merry Tom Lane) to **MR @ 748696**, then **TR** to roundabout on A508. Go **SO** roundabout towards Pitsford Reservoir then keep **SA @** mini roundabout to bottom of the hill and **TL** to join Pitsford Water cycle path. (Bike shop, toilets and café are here)

Pitsford Water – Wansford

Follow cycle path to **MR @ 781702** then **TR** over causeway and follow to **Xroads** in Holcot. **TL** (**SP** Walgrave) and follow round bends until @ **796708**, **TR** onto **BY** and follow to **MR**. **TL** to Walgrave and bear **L** at village green onto High St then **TR** onto Old Rd to soon **FR** onto Newland Rd and follow to **TJ @ 812751**. **TR** then quickly **TL** onto **BW** and follow **NE thru** several gates to join fence lined track, then **MR** to **TJ @ 831768**. **TR** and follow under A43 into Broughton and **TL** onto Cox's Lane to **TJ @ 836762**. Go **SO** onto Gate Lane and bear **L** to **FR** opposite village hall onto good track (**BW**). Descend on track to **TR** and descend steeply to cross bridge over stream and climb to field edge to join good track and follow **BW** to farm to **TL** to **MR @ 861751**. **TL** and follow over A14 then **SO** roundabout into Kettering. @ **873764 TL** to join busy A509 and follow to roundabout @ **876774** then **TR** onto A6003 (Barton Rd). After approx. 300m **TL** onto A6098 (Windmill Ave) then quickly **TR** onto Eastleigh Rd, following round **LH** bend to quickly **TR** over traffic free bridge @ **881776** to join Grantown Close to **TJ** with Kyles Ku Crescent. **TL** and bear **R** to **TJ** with St John's Rd. **TL** and follow to **TJ** with Deeble Rd @ **885785** then **TR** and quickly **TL** (just past bus stop) onto path (**BW**) next to housing estate and follow to join **BW @ 886786**. Continue on singletrack **BW, thru** several gates, to join **MR** in Warkton and follow past church on **R** to **TJ** with **MR** (Pipe Ln) **@ 893799**. TL, cross river then **@ 889802**, **TR** onto **BW** and continue **SA thru** gate to join **MR** (Main St) in Weekly **@ 889806**. Continue **SA** to **TJ** with A4300 and **TR** towards roundabout. Cross road just before roundabout to join cycle path next to busy A4300 and follow past Boughton Park until, **@ 891826 TR** (onto Queens St) into Geddington keeping **SA** over bridge (or ford!) to junction with Queen Eleanor Cross **@ 894830**.

TR onto Grafton Rd then **TL** onto Wood St and follow **SA** to join **BY,** bearing **R @ 899836** to continue to join **MR** and on to Brigstock. **@ 943853 TL** onto Bridge St and follow to **TJ** with High St. **TL**, then **TR** onto Old Dairy Ln and follow to **TJ** with A6116 **@ 946860**. **TL** then quickly **TR** onto **MR** (Old Dairy Ln) and continue **SA** to join **BW** (boggy when wet!). Follow **BW** **N** to **BW** junction **@ 949886**. TR then **TL thru** hedge to continue **N** to **MR @ 953897**. Go **SO** **MR** to join track into airfield then soon after passing trees and **BW** sign on **L**, switchback **L** and follow tall fence line onto **BW** and continue towards mast. Continue on **BW** between fields to join concrete airfield track **@ 953905** and follow until, **@ 960913**, **TL** onto **BW** and descend into Deenethorpe and on to **MR @**

957919. TR and continue until, @ **974913**, TL onto **BW** and descend gradually on good track to **MR** @ **994920**. TL then quickly **TR** onto **BW** and follow up past farm, heading **N** next to woods to descend to good path @ **999935**. TL then @ **BW** junction @ **998938**, **TR thru** gate and continue on **BW** towards Lodge Farm @ **015944**. Just before farm, **TL** and follow **BW** to **MR** then **TL** and continue to **TJ** @ **021958**. TR to **TJ** with **MR** in Apethorpe and **TR** past pub and follow **thru** village, over brook, until, @ **027960**, **TL** onto **BW**. Follow this **thru** woods, past farm and next to fields to **BW** junction @ **038967**. TL and follow **N** until, @ **039971**, **TR**, **thru** gate, onto **BW** and follow faint trail **thru** open fields and several gates until just past woods on **R.** Go **SA thru** gate and quickly **FR** to continue on faint doubletrack **BW** to track junction @ **053974**. **TL** then quickly **FR** to follow **BY N** to join **MR** and keep **SA** until, @ **054984**, **TR** onto **BW** and continue **SA** into Old Sulehay Forest to eventually exit woods onto **MR** @ **068988**. **TL** and descend to **TJ** in Wansford, **TR**, then quickly **TR** onto Bridge End and follow to cross River Nene on old stone bridge into Cambridgeshire which ends this route.

Route Feedback

If you have any local information, for example, trail re-classification, trail closures, bike shops opening or closing or you know of a worthy section of trail that could fit and improve this route then please let us know and it could be included in future editions of 'The Northamptonshire Way'.

Please contact us at **info@mtbepicsuk.co.uk**

Acknowledgements

I'd like to thank my friend Paul who came up with the idea for this route. And to my wife Kathryn and daughter Hannah, for their time and help.

Thanks also to Matt, Shane and Sam for the cover pic.

About the Author

Vince Major lives in Northamptonshire and has been riding mountain bikes since 1989. His broad MTB experiences range from XC, freeride and downhill at home and abroad. His vast knowledge of good MTB areas in the UK stems from the fact that living in Northants, not being a MTB hotspot itself, has meant travelling to other areas to find and ride the best trails. This has eventually prompted him to write a series of long distance route guides.

Vince has also acquired a wealth of experience in organising single and multi-day bike events all over the UK, with the emphasis on 'having an adventure'.

Other books in the
by Mountain Bike series

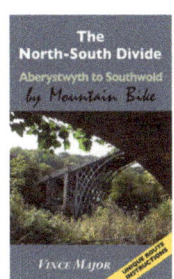

Please contact Vince Major at:
info@mtbepicsuk.co.uk

Lightning Source UK Ltd.
Milton Keynes UK
UKHW051320160621
385595UK00007B/73